English # Heritage
Illustrated Souvenir Guide

stonehenge

and neighbouring monuments

Text by

R J C Atkinson MA FSA

Formerly Professor of Archaeology,
University College, Cardiff

London:
Historic Buildings & Monuments
Commission for England

contents

The stonehenge area

The landscape for a few miles around Stonehenge contains more prehistoric remains than any other area of the same size in Britain. This guide describes and illustrates the principal monuments and explains their significance. Their positions are shown on the map, and the table on p4 gives their dates.

These dates are based mainly on the radiocarbon process, which can measure the age of specimens of animal or vegetable material found in excavations, usually in the form of wood charcoal, animal bones or deer antlers. Dates obtained in this way are rough ones only, with a margin of uncertainty of several centuries either way. They do allow us, however, to arrange the various monuments more or less in the order in which they were built and used. Because of recent improvements in the radiocarbon dating process, most of the dates given in this guide are several centuries earlier than those previously published.

The monuments themselves are of several different kinds, with different purposes. The most numerous – the long barrows of the Neolithic period and the round barrows of the Beaker period and the Early Bronze Age – are burial places. The 'causewayed camp' at Robin Hood Ball is probably a ceremonial enclosure for tribal meetings. The Cursus seems to be a ritual enclosure of another sort, perhaps for processions or races. The three 'henge monuments' – Stonehenge, Woodhenge and Durrington Walls – are generally thought to be prehistoric temples, though we shall never know how they were used or what religious beliefs they represent. No prehistoric houses or other domestic sites have so far been found in the area, but there is a group of flint mines close to Durrington Walls.

Most of these monuments have been partially excavated at various times over the last two centuries. As a result of these explorations, and of similar ones elsewhere, it is possible to describe in outline the way of life of the people who built and used them. Because the monuments belong to the prehistoric period, however, long before any written records were made, there are many questions about them that we shall never be able to answer. The evidence consists of fragmentary remains of structures, long ruined and decayed, and mostly underground, and of objects of stone, metal, pottery and bone, many of them no more than scraps of former rubbish. Wood, leather, cloth and other organic materials have all vanished. The archaeologist can now study only a small and very incomplete part of what originally existed.

From this evidence it is often possible to say *how* things were made or built, and in some cases to tell *when* and *by whom*. It is hardly ever possible to answer the question *why*.

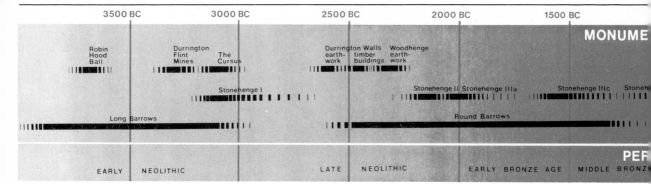

	3500 BC	3000 BC	2500 BC	2000 BC	1500 BC

MONUME

Robin Hood Ball

Durrington Flint Mines   The Cursus

Durrington Walls earth-work   Woodhenge earth-work   timber buildings

Stonehenge I

Stonehenge II   Stonehenge IIIa   Stonehenge IIIc   Stoneh

Long Barrows

Round Barrows

PER

| EARLY | NEOLITHIC | | LATE | NEOLITHIC | EARLY BRONZE AGE | MIDDLE BRONZ |

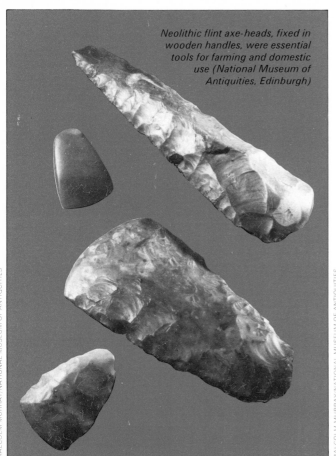

Neolithic flint axe-heads, fixed in wooden handles, were essential tools for farming and domestic use (National Museum of Antiquities, Edinburgh)

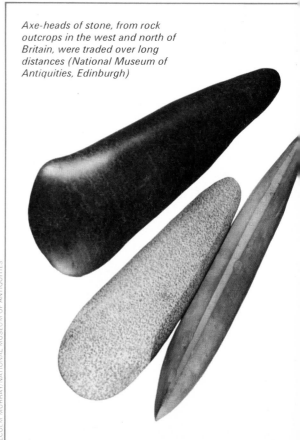

Axe-heads of stone, from rock outcrops in the west and north of Britain, were traded over long distances (National Museum of Antiquities, Edinburgh)

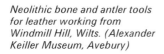

Neolithic bone and antler tools for leather working from Windmill Hill, Wilts. (Alexander Keiller Museum, Avebury)

The prehistoric people

For many thousands of years, up to about 4000BC, the people living in the area consisted of a few scattered bands of roving hunters living on game, fish from the rivers and wild plants. They grew no crops and had no domesticated animals. For tools and weapons they used flint, bone and deer antler, and for shelter they built huts or wind-breaks of brushwood at their temporary camp-sites, and perhaps used skin tents as well.

The landscape at this time was very different from that of today, with broad tracts of dense woodland and hardly any open grassland. It could support only a tiny population of hunters, so that probably no more than a single family lived in the area covered by the map.

About 4000BC the southern and eastern parts of Britain began to be colonised by small groups of early farming settlers, coming from the coasts of Europe across the Channel and the North Sea in skin boats. They brought with them their own seed corn (mainly a primitive form of wheat) and small numbers of domesticated beasts – cattle, sheep, goats and pigs – from which to build up new flocks and herds in their new homeland. They settled in various areas, including the chalk of Wessex and especially Salisbury Plain, where their remains are more numerous than elsewhere.

They seem to have led a simple and peaceful peasant life, herding their beasts in the forests (where the animals atè leaves rather than grass) and growing grain in small irregular plots, cleared of scrub by felling with flint axes and burning the brushwood and undergrowth. The ground was tilled with digging-sticks and a primitive wooden plough, and the same plots were probably sown with a crop year after year until the fertility of the soil was exhausted. Then the families concerned would move away to a new area, and clear new plots from the forest and scrub. No houses of this period survive for certain in Wiltshire, but from discoveries elsewhere we know that they were log-cabins the size of a large modern room and thus big enough for a single family only.

Their tools and hunting weapons were mostly of flint, which they mined by digging shafts into the chalk. For axes, specially important for the clearing of woodland and the shaping of timber for houses, they also used other kinds of rock imported from axe-factories as far distant as Cumbria, North Wales and Cornwall. Many small implements were made of bone and antler. Their clothes were of leather (like the suede used today), and hide was probably used for some of their domestic utensils. Their baggy round-bottomed pots look like imitations in clay of the leather vessels appropriate to a pastoral people. They buried their dead under long barrows.

After the first settlement these early Neolithic farmers probably grew in numbers fairly quickly, because unlike the native hunters, who had to live from hand to mouth, they

5

Above: *Neolithic pots from Abingdon, Oxfordshire (Ashmolean Museum, Oxford)*

could build up a store of surplus food in the form of grain and of meat on the hoof. In time this increased population had a marked effect on the landscape, through the replacement of forest by open grassland and by thickets of scrub. This was brought about partly by the deliberate clearance of woodland, but mainly by prolonged grazing in the forests. Trees were stripped of their leaves to feed cattle, goats nibbled the bark of young saplings and pigs grubbed up their roots, so that when old trees died they were not replaced by new ones. By Late Neolithic times, from about 3000BC, much of the original forest had disappeared and the landscape was beginning to resemble the sparsely-wooded open grassland of today. By this time too the population had grown so much that labour could be spared for 'public works'.

Soon after 2500BC new groups of immigrants crossed the North Sea from Holland and the Rhineland and settled in small numbers in eastern and southern Britain. They are known as the Beaker people from the common occurrence of pottery drinking-vessels in their graves. They seem to have had a good deal of influence on the way of life of the native British population of Neolithic farmers, partly perhaps because they introduced the working and use of the first metals, copper and gold. The main sources of these lay in Ireland, and it was probably the Beaker people who opened up trade routes to Wessex and other parts of Britain and thus laid the foundations of a British bronze industry which was to last for nearly two thousand years.

A new custom introduced by the Beaker people, and widely adopted by the native population, was the burial of the dead singly under a round mound or barrow, with a beaker or drinking-vessel and sometimes with a copper knife or a bow and arrows tipped with flint. From this time onwards, up to the end of the Early Bronze Age about 1500BC, burial under a round barrow became the almost universal practice for people of importance, and one nowhere better seen than in the landscape round Stonehenge.

The Beaker people, though small in numbers, seem to have maintained their own distinctive customs and way of life for several centuries after their first settlement in Britain, but gradually and probably by intermarriage they mixed with the native Neolithic population and thus began to lose their own special identity. In much the same way the Norman invaders of England, originally distinct with their own language and customs, gradually mixed with the English and in so doing changed both their way of life and their speech. It may well be (though we shall never know for certain) that it was the Beaker people who introduced the British language which persisted up to the coming of the Saxons and survives today as Welsh.

By about 2000BC the growing use of bronze for tools and weapons, made by alloying copper from the west of Britain and from

Objects from the burial of a Wessex chieftain in Bush Barrow, near Stonehenge. Below and right: *gold plates and scabbard-hook, and daggers of copper and bronze (Devizes Museum)*

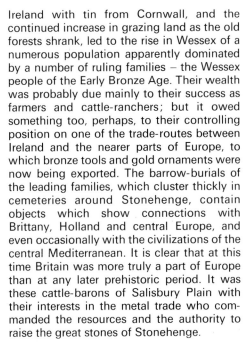

Left and below: *bone-inlaid wand, stone mace-head (found separately) and bronze axe-head, from the same grave (Devizes Museum)*

Ireland with tin from Cornwall, and the continued increase in grazing land as the old forests shrank, led to the rise in Wessex of a numerous population apparently dominated by a number of ruling families – the Wessex people of the Early Bronze Age. Their wealth was probably due mainly to their success as farmers and cattle-ranchers; but it owed something too, perhaps, to their controlling position on one of the trade-routes between Ireland and the nearer parts of Europe, to which bronze tools and gold ornaments were now being exported. The barrow-burials of the leading families, which cluster thickly in cemeteries around Stonehenge, contain objects which show connections with Brittany, Holland and central Europe, and even occasionally with the civilizations of the central Mediterranean. It is clear that at this time Britain was more truly a part of Europe than at any later prehistoric period. It was these cattle-barons of Salisbury Plain with their interests in the metal trade who commanded the resources and the authority to raise the great stones of Stonehenge.

At the end of the Early Bronze Age, about 1500BC, this rich community seems to have suffered a rapid decline. Signs of wealth and aristocracy disappear, and surplus labour was no longer used for great public works. Instead there seems to have been a return to a simple peasant way of life which was to persist for nearly a thousand years. The reasons for this change are unknown, though perhaps the beginnings of a worsening of the climate may have had something to do with it, together with the adoption of a new pattern of farming. The growing of grain, mainly barley, on fields with permanent boundaries, and the use of manure to restore the fertility of soils cultivated on some kind of rotation of crops, probably reduced the amount of spare time that could have been used for 'public works'. It is clear that after about 1500BC the Stonehenge region as a whole began to lose the special importance as a centre of religion and of political power which it had possessed for the last two thousand years.

After this date, only a very few round barrows were added to the long-established cemeteries which lie all around Stonehenge, and no new major monuments were built. None the less, the Stonehenge Avenue was extended about 1100BC, which must mean that Stonehenge itself was still in use, both then and for some unknown period afterwards, and that it retained its special importance. No other prehistoric monument in Britain has so long a history of continuous use, despite the many changes that must have taken place in the economy and social structure, and perhaps even in the religious beliefs, of the people who used it.

The monument:

To give the reader as complete a picture as possible, all the major prehistoric monuments of the Neolithic period and the beginning of the Bronze Age in the Stonehenge area are described and illustrated in this Guide. Some of them, however, including many of the long and round barrows, lie on private land or in a military area and cannot be visited by the public.

ASHMOLEAN MUSEUM

Robin Hood Ball

The Long Barrows

: Robin Hood Ball, a ~hic causewayed camp, ~e air

This eroded earthwork lies on a slight rise in the chalk downland about 4.3km (2.7 miles) north-north-west of Stonehenge, in a military area closed to the public. Two irregular rings of bank and ditch enclose an oval space of about 1 hectare (2.5 acres), both ditches being broken by unexcavated causeways of solid chalk.

This is probably the earliest prehistoric site in the area, and the only local example of a Neolithic 'causewayed camp', of which about thirty have been found on the chalk and the valley gravels of southern and eastern England. They seem to date from about 4000 to 3300BC, and they probably served as tribal meeting-places. In some of them rubbish deliberately buried in the ditches may be the remains of ceremonial feasts. Other rubbish includes scraps of pottery and broken stone axes which were made more than 160km (100 miles) away. This suggests that causewayed camps may have been used, amongst other things, for the exchange of goods by barter, and perhaps too for other tribal purposes, which today would be served by the town hall, the magistrates' court and even, possibly, by the church or chapel.

The limited excavations at Robin Hood Ball have not shown whether there were buildings within the enclosure; but we can be fairly sure that this was the first 'community centre' in the area, long before anything was built at Stonehenge.

~erial view of the cemetery ~nd barrows at ~bourne Stoke cross-roads, ~n earlier long barrow at the west end (bottom left)

Throughout the chalk of Wessex and Sussex, and further north in Lincolnshire and east Yorkshire, the early Neolithic farmers buried their dead in long barrows, of which over 200 are known in these areas. Fifteen of them lie within a radius of about 5km (3 miles) of Stonehenge, a larger number than in any area of the same size elsewhere. This suggests that the neighbourhood was one of special importance or sanctity even before Stonehenge itself was built.

The long barrows of the area vary in length from 20m (65ft) to 80m (265ft), and all but one of them exceeds 30m (100ft). Their width varies even more, but is usually between one-sixth and one-third of the length, as originally built. Allowance must be made for the spreading of the mound sideways as the result of thousands of years of weathering and erosion. Originally the mounds of chalk, excavated from ditches with flat bottoms and almost vertical sides, parallel with the edges of the barrow, stood up to 3m (10ft) in height. In some cases the sides of the mound were parallel, and in others one end was broader and higher than the other.

Many of the long barrows in the area were partially excavated in the nineteenth century, but the records of these explorations do not allow us to reconstruct the ritual of burial. More recent excavations elsewhere, however, show that the bodies of the dead were kept above ground for some time, and in some cases were exposed on raised timber plat-

Flint-mining tools from Easton Down, Wiltshire: pick-axe and rake of red deer antler, and cow shoulder-blade used as a scraper for rubble (Salisbury Museum)

Flint mines

forms where they would be out of reach of animals but would soon be picked clean by birds of prey. Only after some years, and perhaps when some one of special importance had died, were the bones collected and laid on the ground, sometimes inside a low mortuary building of timber. Then the long mound of chalk was piled over them, the bones lying towards one end which usually faced roughly towards the east.

The best-preserved long barrow in the area lies on private land just to the north-east of the roundabout at the Winterbourne Stoke cross-roads, on the A303 about 2.4km (1.5 miles) from Stonehenge. It can be seen by walking along the northern verge of the road to the east of the roundabout. This long barrow is typical of its kind in Wessex. It contains over 1500 cubic metres (53 000 cubic feet) of chalk. With the primitive tools available it would have taken a dozen people about four months to build, if they worked for eight hours every day.

None of the long barrows in the area has been dated directly, but examples elsewhere in Wessex suggest that they were built between about 4000BC and 3000BC. We cannot tell whether a long barrow was the tomb of all the members of a single family (apart from children who died very young), or whether it was used only for the burial of selected people of special importance, belonging to a group of neighbouring or related families. Future studies may solve this problem.

The main material used for tools and hunting weapons by the Neolithic farmers was flint, which occurs at various levels in the chalk in the form of seams of large lumps or nodules. Near the surface it has been cracked by frost during the Ice Age and is useless for making tools, so that suitable material had to be mined by sinking shafts into the chalk.

In 1952 a sewer-trench to the north-east of Durrington Walls (p36) cut through part of a flint-mining area. Three broad shallow pits had evidently been dug to exploit a seam of flint very close to the surface, which was probably of poor quality. Two other shafts had been dug to a depth of 2.2m (7.2ft), with low galleries extending from the bottom to follow a deeper seam. The full extent of this mining area is unknown, and the site is now covered by houses and gardens. In view of the importance of the Stonehenge area there may well be other flint-mines in the neighbourhood which still await discovery.

the cursus

*: the Cursus, as engraved
keley's Stonehenge
, with the Avenue and the
in the distance

This extraordinary earthwork lies about 800m (875 yards) to the north of Stonehenge. It consists of a narrow enclosure 2.8km (1.75 miles) long and 90m (100 yards) wide, marked out on either side by a small bank with a ditch outside, much of which has been flattened by ploughing. To the west, just beyond Fargo Plantation, it was closed by a rounded end where the ditch and bank were deeper and higher than elsewhere. To the east it was aligned on a long barrow of earlier date, which has been worn away by a modern track which passes over it. The small part which survives cannot, at the time of writing, be visited by the public.

Elsewhere in southern and eastern England a number of similar earthworks have been discovered. Some of these are also aligned on earlier long barrows, and some have been firmly dated to the Late Neolithic period by excavation. Their purpose is unknown; but their unusual shape suggests that they were ceremonial or religious enclosures, intended perhaps for processions or for ritual races connected with the honouring of dead ancestors.

The name 'Cursus' was first given to this earthwork by the eighteenth-century anti-quary William Stukeley, who thought that it was a race-course for the chariots of the Ancient Britons. We know now that it is of much earlier date, and that it may have been the religious centre of the Stonehenge area before Stonehenge itself was built.

To the west of Fargo Plantation there are the remains of a much smaller Cursus, now almost invisible, which is rounded at the west end, open at the east end and divided in the centre by a transverse ditch. It is shorter than most of the other Cursus monuments, and it has not been excavated, so that its date and purpose are unknown. It lies on private land, not open to visitors.

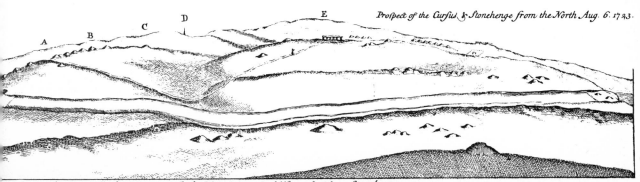

Prospect of the Cursus & Stonehenge from the North Aug. 6. 1723.

A *Entrance of the Avenue*. B. *The 7 Barrows*. C. *The Kings Barrow*. D. *Salisbury Steeple*. E *Stonehenge*.

stonehenge

Stonehenge is the most important prehistoric monument in the area, and indeed in the whole of Britain. It is unique, and there is nothing else like it anywhere in the world. From the earliest times it has aroused the awe and the curiosity of its visitors. It was first mentioned as one of the wonders of Britain only seventy years after the Norman conquest, and since then almost every people of antiquity has been claimed as its builders, at one time or another.

It is only during the twentieth century that archaeological excavations have yielded reliable information about its history and its age, so that we can now say what the main features of Stonehenge are, and roughly when and in what order they were built.

The outer boundary of Stonehenge is the low circular *bank* which lies about 30m (100ft) outside the stones. Originally it stood about 1.8m (6ft) high and was built of chalk rubble quarried from the *ditch* immediately outside it. In the course of nearly fifty centuries most of it has been weathered down and has slipped back, obscuring the very irregular outlines of the ditch, which originally consisted of a string of rough quarry-pits with steep sides and flat bottoms. One half of the circuit of the ditch was excavated in 1919–26, and was only partly refilled afterwards. The other half remains untouched.

The earthwork is broken by a broad *entrance* on the north-east side, nearest the road, and by some smaller gaps elsewhere, some of

15

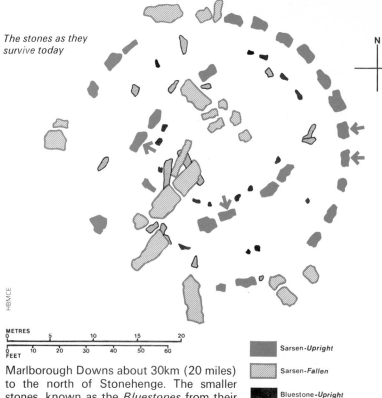

The stones as they survive today

N

HBMCE

METRES
0   5   10   15   20

FEET
0   10   20   30   40   50   60

Sarsen-*Upright*

Sarsen-*Fallen*

Bluestone-*Upright*

Bluestone-*Fallen*

← *Carvings on stones*

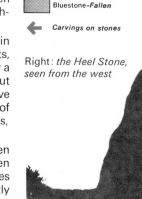

Right: *the Heel Stone, seen from the west*

which are modern. From the entrance the *Avenue*, marked by a low bank and ditch on either side, runs downhill across the road and leads eventually to the bank of the River Avon at West Amesbury. Within the Avenue, close to the road, stands the *Heel Stone* with traces of a circular ditch around its base.

Just inside the bank is a ring of 56 pits, now filled up, known as the *Aubrey Holes* after their discoverer John Aubrey (1626–97). About half of them have been excavated and are marked by discs of white cement let into the turf.

At the entrance of the earthwork is a large fallen stone, known as the *Slaughter Stone*. It originally stood upright on its outer end and together with a similar stone, now vanished, formed a ceremonial doorway to the site. Further round the earthwork, on the line of the Aubrey Holes, there are two smaller stones, one fallen and one still upright, called the *Station Stones*. Two other stones, now missing, formerly stood at a similar distance inside the bank, each of them in a small ditched enclosure. These are known as the North and South Barrows, though there was no central mound. Only the South Barrow has been excavated.

The standing stones in the centre consist of two main kinds of rock. The larger blocks and their lintels, with the Station Stones, Slaughter Stone and Heel Stone, are all of *sarsen*, a natural sandstone which occurs as huge boulders on the surface of the

Marlborough Downs about 30km (20 miles) to the north of Stonehenge. The smaller stones, known as the *Bluestones* from their colour, are of several kinds of rock which come from the Preseli Mountains in south-west Wales.

The *Sarsen Circle*, about 30m (100ft) in diameter, consisted originally of 30 uprights, each weighing about 25 tonnes, capped by a continuous ring of 30 lintels weighing about 7 tonnes. Inside it was a horseshoe of five *Sarsen Trilithons* each consisting of a pair of huge uprights, weighing up to 45 tonnes, capped by a massive lintel.

Apart from the Heel Stone and the fallen Station Stone, all the sarsens have been dressed to shape by pounding their surfaces with stone hammers. The uprights are slightly 'dished' on the top to provide a secure seating for the lintels, and tenons have been left

Right: *the first trilithon and part of the bluestone horseshoe*

Far right: *battered tenon on a bluestone pillar in the horseshoe*

GATEWAY FILM PRODUCTIONS

R J C ATKINSON

R J C ATKINSON

projecting from them to fit into corresponding hollow mortice-holes in the undersides of the lintels. In addition the lintels of the outer circle are fitted to each other with vertical tongue-and-groove joints.

The *Bluestone Circle*, now much ruined and incomplete, stands inside the sarsen circle. Originally it consisted of about 60 stones set close together. Only two of the surviving stones have been dressed to shape, and both of these had formerly been used as lintels.

The *Bluestone Horseshoe*, standing inside the sarsen horseshoe, originally had 19 stones which increased in height towards the centre. They have all been dressed to one of two shapes, a square pillar or a tapering obelisk, which alternate round the horseshoe. Two of them bear traces on their tops of projecting tenons, which have been almost battered away. Another has a dished top, like the sarsen uprights, and the adjacent pillar has a groove worked all the way down one side. This stone must once have fitted against another with a corresponding ridge, which now survives only as a stump below the surface on the opposite side of the horseshoe.

At the focus of the bluestone horseshoe is the *Altar Stone*, a dressed block of blue-grey sandstone from the shores of Milford Haven in Pembrokeshire, about 5m (16ft) long. It is now buried in the ground beneath the fallen upright and lintel of the great sarsen trilithon, but originally it probably stood upright as a pillar.

GATEWAY FILM PRODUCTIONS

Above: *traces of a tenon on a fallen bluestone pillar*

Below: *the sarsen circle from outside*

HBMCE

In addition to these visible features, there are two settings of pits discovered in excavations but not marked on the surface. The *Y* and *Z Holes* form two circles about 11m (36ft) and 3.7m (12ft) outside the sarsen circle. There are thirty pits in the Y ring but only 29 in the Z ring. One Z hole on the west side lies beneath a fallen sarsen, and another to the south-east is missing altogether. The *Q* and *R Holes* form the ends of a series of dumbbell-shaped trenches, radially aligned and each about 1.9m (6ft) long, the centres of which lie beneath the circumference of the present bluestone circle. They originally held bluestones in two concentric circles, about 22.5m (74ft) and 26.2m (86ft) across. The stones left impressions of their bases in the holes, and in some of these small chips of bluestone remained embedded after their removal.

The History of Stonehenge

As in many later cathedrals and churches, not all the structures that we see today at Stonehenge were built at the same time. As the result of excavations we can now divide the history of Stonehenge into several periods, covering a span of about twenty centuries between about 3100 and 1100BC.

Period I. The earliest structures were the bank and ditch, the Heel Stone and the Aubrey Holes, all probably built about 3100BC. There was probably some kind of gateway or ceremonial arch of timber a little to the west of the Heel Stone, on the axis of symmetry of the circular earthwork, and a pair of small stones standing in the middle of the entrance, forming a doorway without a lintel. Perhaps too there was some small building of timber, or a setting of stones, at the centre, an area long since destroyed by treasure-hunters.

The Aubrey Holes are round pits in the chalk about one metre wide and deep, with steep sides and flat bottoms, forming a circle about 86.6m (284ft) in diameter. They seem to have been filled up very soon after they were dug. Later, cremated human bones were buried in smaller holes made in the chalk filling; but there is no reason to suppose that they were made as graves in the first place, or that they ever held uprights of wood or stone. They probably represent some kind of magical or religious ceremony, of which we shall never know the details.

It is possible that the four Station Stones belong to this period also, but the evidence is uncertain.

A few similar open-air temples of much smaller size, containing rings of pits with cremated burials, have been found elsewhere in Britain. Like the first Stonehenge they all probably belong to the Late Neolithic period.

Period II. After nine or more centuries, Stonehenge was radically remodelled, around 2100BC. About 80 bluestones, weighing up to 4 tonnes apiece, were to be set up in the Q and R Holes to form two circles, one inside the other, round the centre of the site. There was an entrance, pointing towards the rising sun at mid-summer, marked by extra stones on the inside; and on the opposite side a large pit may have held a bluestone of exceptional size, perhaps the present Altar Stone. There was also some kind of interior setting, possibly a horseshoe, of which only a few holes are known. The bluestones were probably brought to Stonehenge from some undiscovered site in Wiltshire to which they had been transported centuries before for another purpose. Excavations have shown, however, that this double circle was never finished and that for at least a quarter of its circumference on the west side the stones were not set up.

At the same time the original entrance of the circular earthwork was widened to match the new axis, by throwing about 8m (25ft) of the bank back into the ditch on the east side. From here the nearer part of the Avenue was built

The development of stonehenge

These bird's-eye views show the development of Stonehenge over about 1,300 years, and are based on the result of excavations and radio-carbon dating. In Period I there were two stones in the entrance, with the Heel Stone and a timber gateway outside. In Period II a double circle of bluestones (unfinished) and the Avenue were added. In Period IIIa the sarsens replaced the bluestones, and in Period IIIb some bluestones were erected inside the circle, and the Y and Z Holes were dug but never used. Finally in Period IIIc (opposite) the bluestones were re-arranged in a circle and a horseshoe

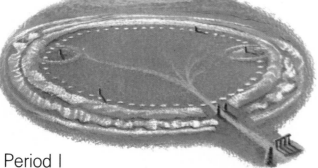

Period I
about 3100 BC

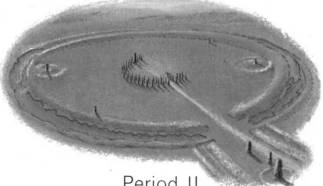

Period II
about 2100 BC

Period IIIa
about 2000 BC

Period IIIb
date uncertain

Below: *the side of this sarsen has*
dressed by hammering shallow gr
to remove the rough surface
natural

on the same sunrise alignment, and the Heel Stone was enclosed by a narrow ditch, almost at once filled up again.

This remodelling of Stonehenge was probably the work of the Beaker people (p7). It looks as if the building of the double bluestone circle was still in progress when the decision was made, for reasons that we shall never know, to abandon it and to replace it by something much larger.

Period IIIa. This new structure, probably started about 2000BC, was the lintelled circle and horseshoe of large sarsen stones, whose remains we can still see today. Its axis, like that of the unfinished double circle which it replaced, pointed to the midsummer sunrise and was further marked by a pair of large stones set close together in the entrance of the earthwork, only one of which, the fallen Slaughter Stone, now survives.

This extraordinary building exhibits a number of refinements which cannot be found anywhere else amongst the prehistoric stone monuments of Europe, outside the Mediterranean area. First, all the stones have been squared and dressed to shape by pounding their surfaces with heavy stone hammers before they were erected. Second, the lintels are held in place on their uprights by mortice-and-tenon joints, worked in the solid stone, and the lintels of the outer circle are locked end-to-end by vertical tongue-and-groove joints as well. Thirdly, the lintels

themselves are not straight-sided blocks, but have their sides shaped to the curves on which they lie. Furthermore, the sides of the trilithon lintels are not vertical but are inclined towards the ground. These are all refinements of design which are peculiar to Stonehenge alone.

The jointing of the stones is probably imitated from woodworking methods, and we know that at much the same date huge timber structures were being erected close by at Woodhenge (p34) and Durrington Walls (p36). The upward taper of the sarsen pillars may likewise imitate the natural tapering form of tree-trunks; but it could possibly represent a deliberate though crude attempt to increase the apparent height of the stones by an optical illusion. Similarly the tilting of the sides of the trilithon lintels does have the effect, and perhaps intentionally, of making them look as if they were vertical to an observer inside the horseshoe.

Given the size and weight of the stones, and the primitive means available for moving, shaping and erecting them, this sarsen building of the Early Bronze Age represents one of the most remarkable and astonishing of all the achievements of prehistoric man in Europe.

Period IIIb. After the sarsen stones had been set up, rather more than twenty of the bluestones dismantled at the end of period II were selected, dressed to shape and erected in

R J C ATKINSON

Right: *this tenon on the tallest upright was made by pounding away the stone around it*

: *the lintels are shaped to rve of the sarsen circle*

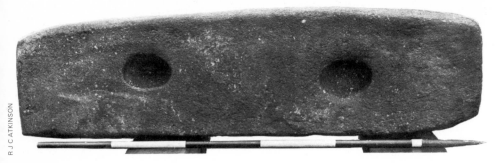

Left: *the underside of one of the bluestone lintels, showing the mortice holes*

an oval setting on the line of the later bluestone horseshoe. Only a few of the stone-holes for this setting have so far been found in excavations, so that its exact plan is still uncertain. It does seem to have included, however, at least two miniature copies in bluestone of the great sarsen trilithons and the tongued-and-grooved pair, the separate components of which still survive, though re-used in a different way at a later date. One of the two bluestone lintels, now in the present bluestone circle, has marks of wear on its under side which show that it must have rested on its supporting pillar for a long time, perhaps for several centuries.

We do not know the date of this oval setting of dressed bluestones. It could have been part of the same design as the sarsen stones, and completed as soon as they had been set up. Equally, it could have been a fresh addition at a later date. In either case, however, it seems to have been the intention of the builders to make use in the end of the remaining 60 bluestones left over from period II, which had not so far been dressed to shape. It is almost certainly to hold these that the two rings of Y and Z Holes were dug about 1550BC, to form once again a double circle.

For some unknown reason, however, this project too was abandoned unfinished. The last few holes to be dug, on the east side, were irregular and incomplete, and no stones were ever set up in any of them. The design was abandoned, and the oval setting of blue-stones in the centre was demolished.

Period IIIc. The final reconstruction of Stonehenge probably followed almost at once. The uprights of the former oval structure were reset in the horseshoe of bluestones that we can see the remains of today, and probably reshaped to their present alternating forms of pillar and obelisk. The remaining unshaped bluestones were erected in the present blue-stone circle, together with the two bluestone lintels, re-used as pillars with the mortice-holes facing outwards so that they could not be seen from inside. Both have since fallen over in different directions, so that the mortices on one of them now lie under-ground. The original number of stones in the bluestone circle was probably about 60, set quite close together, but most of them have since been broken up or removed, or survive only as battered stumps below ground level.

The largest bluestone of all, the Altar Stone, probably stood as a tall pillar on the axial line inside the central and highest sarsen trilithon, and has since fallen down. There is no reason to suppose that its present position, or its name, is more than accidental.

Period IV. About 1100BC the Avenue was extended from Stonehenge Bottom to pass over the hill to the east, and from there south-eastwards to the River Avon. This must mean that Stonehenge was still in use at that date, and presumably for some time afterwards, but we do not know how long.

Above: *stumps of stones in the bluestone circle, found in excavations*

Right: *this tongued bluestone stump, below ground level, clearly once fitted against the grooved bluestone (below)*

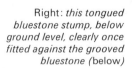

Right: *the trilithon lintels are gently curved and their sides are inclined outwards*

The Later History. The final reconstruction of Stonehenge itself took place at the end of the Early Bronze Age, about 1550BC, and its subsequent history is one of ruin, damage and destruction. In spite of their great size, many of the sarsen stones have disappeared. We know, however, that their builders were trying to achieve the maximum overall height with the material available, so that many of them stood in dangerously shallow holes and probably fell over at an early date. Moreover, there is no natural building stone within 21km (13 miles) of Stonehenge, so that in the Middle Ages, if not before, the fallen stones and the lintels (which could be levered or pulled off their uprights fairly easily) must have provided a convenient quarry for local builders.

The disappearance of so many of the blue-stones, or their survival only as stumps below ground level, is easy to understand, because they are smaller and more brittle than the sarsens, and thus easier to pull down or break up with hammers. Much of the destruction is certainly due to earlier visitors, who delighted in knocking off fragments as keepsakes. Indeed at one time a hammer could be readily hired at the blacksmith's forge in Amesbury for this very purpose. It is known too that up to about a century ago the local farmers used to break up the bluestones and the fallen sarsens for road metal, to repair farm tracks and gateways.

Until 1918, when it was given to the nation, Stonehenge was in private hands. Since that date about half of the site has been excavated at various times, and a number of the leaning and fallen stones have been straightened and re-erected. In recent years the number of visitors has become so large (three-quarters of a million in a year) that the surface of the monument, right out to the surrounding bank and ditch, has been dangerously eroded, and many of the fallen stones, and the stumps which protrude above the surface, are being ground away by the feet of those who step or climb on them. It has thus become necessary to prevent further erosion by restricting public access to the interior of the site. Only in this way can this unique structure be preserved for the future.

The Carvings on the Sarsen Stones. Four of the sarsen uprights have prehistoric carvings on their sides. The earliest of these, high up on the inside face of the fourth trilithon of the horseshoe, is a shallow oblong shape similar to carvings found in Neolithic stone burial-chambers in Brittany, which are sometimes thought to represent in a simplified and symbolic way the figure of a mother-goddess. This carving is out of reach of the ground and was therefore made, probably, before the stone was set up.

The carvings on the other three stones are all nearer the ground, and made after the stones had been erected. Most of them are full-size representations of bronze axe-heads of the

STUART PIGGOTT

: carvings of axe-heads dagger, eroded by ering

Below: *the shallow angular carving on the fourth trilithon, resembling 'mother-goddess' symbols in Brittany*

MALCOLM MURRAY

Early Bronze Age, of a kind commonly made in Britain and Ireland between 1800BC and 1500BC; but there is one carving also of a bronze dagger, the details of which are unlike those of contemporary British weapons. It could represent a foreign dagger, of the kind found in the Shaft Graves of Mycenae in Greece, the royal tombs of the legendary home of Agamemnon, dated between 1600BC and 1500BC. At least one of the Early Bronze Age barrows near Stonehenge provides evidence of a similar link at the same date; but this identification of the carving at Stonehenge must remain a matter of opinion.

We shall never know for certain the reason for these carvings, but we can guess that these bronze weapons had some special significance as symbols, just as on many recent war-memorials a bronze sword stands both for the fallen soldier and for the Christian cross. All of them are now much weathered by time; but it is clear that they were shaped by abrasion with small stone hammers, much as the surfaces of the sarsen stones had themselves earlier been dressed smooth. Sarsen stone is far too hard to be cut with bronze chisels.

Astronomy at Stonehenge. Ever since the early eighteenth century it has been recognised that the axis of the sarsen stones (period IIIa) points roughly to where an observer at the centre of Stonehenge would see the sun rise on the longest day of the year, in its most northerly position on the horizon.

ANTONY MILES

We know now, moreover, that this direction formed the axis of Stonehenge even earlier, in period II.

More recently it has been suggested that the lines joining the four Station Stones could also have marked the most northerly and southerly positions on the horizon of the risings and settings of the sun and the moon, and that the latitude of Stonehenge was chosen so that pairs of these directions would be at right angles. In addition, the theory has been advanced that the ring of Aubrey Holes could have been used as a simplified model of the motions of the sun and moon, so as to predict eclipses; and it has also been claimed that Stonehenge served as an observatory for very precise observations of the extreme risings and settings of the moon.

Studies of other stone circles in Britain do suggest that their builders in Late Neolithic and Early Bronze Age times may have had a surprisingly exact knowledge of the way in which the directions of the risings and settings of the sun and moon vary with time. We cannot therefore reject out of hand the idea that the builders of Stonehenge used parts of it to mark and to record similar observations. We must admit, however, that Stonehenge is today so ruined that it is no longer possible to recover with certainty the sight-lines to the horizon that may have been built into it originally. The use of Stonehenge as an astronomical observatory in prehistoric times must remain a matter of speculation.

V & A MUSEUM

Top: *seventeenth-century engraving by David Loggan (Salisbury Museum)*

Centre: *John Constable's watercolour of 1835 (Victoria & Albert Museum, London)*

The Druids

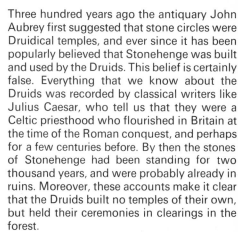

Three hundred years ago the antiquary John Aubrey first suggested that stone circles were Druidical temples, and ever since it has been popularly believed that Stonehenge was built and used by the Druids. This belief is certainly false. Everything that we know about the Druids was recorded by classical writers like Julius Caesar, who tell us that they were a Celtic priesthood who flourished in Britain at the time of the Roman conquest, and perhaps for a few centuries before. By then the stones of Stonehenge had been standing for two thousand years, and were probably already in ruins. Moreover, these accounts make it clear that the Druids built no temples of their own, but held their ceremonies in clearings in the forest.

It may be, however, that the Druids inherited the knowledge and observations of natural events, astronomy included, of the builders of Stonehenge, handed down over the centuries by word of mouth. We are told that the Druids' lore was enshrined in a series of interminable verses, which a novice might take up to twenty years to learn by heart. Since there is no evidence from prehistoric Britain for any method of writing, or of writing down numbers, this is one way in which such knowledge could have been stored and then passed on from one generation to the next. We know, for instance, that in the Pacific today accurate sailing-directions for very long voyages have been handed down by word of mouth alone over a period of many centuries.

PICTUREPOINT

29

In this aerial view the buried ditches of the Avenue show as darker lines in a growing crop, on the hill east of Stonehenge

The Avenue

The Avenue provides the approach to Stonehenge and links it to the bank of the River Avon at West Amesbury, some 2.5km (1.5 miles) away to the east-south-east. It is marked on the ground by two parallel ditches with banks on the inside. From the entrance to Stonehenge it passes the Heel Stone and runs downhill for about 530m (1740ft) to the dry valley called Stonehenge Bottom. About half way down it is crossed by a similar pair of low parallel banks, without ditches, which have sometimes mistakenly been thought to be prehistoric. They are in fact the remains of an old road from Amesbury to Shrewton, which was in use up to 150 years ago.

Beyond the dry valley the Avenue has long since been destroyed by ploughing, and its course was rediscovered by air-photography only about fifty years ago. In the valley bottom it swings sharply eastwards, and climbs the slope to pass between the two beech woods on the skyline. There it curves round to the south-east and then runs straight down the slope to the river. Its total length is about 2,780m (3,040 yards).

The straight section nearest to Stonehenge has been dated by the radiocarbon method to about 2100BC and belongs to period II, when the alignment on the midsummer sunrise was first adopted. The more distant sections are less accurately set out, with a varying width, and were added about 1100BC. By then the first section, built a thousand years before, was much eroded but still visible.

ASHMOLEAN MUSEUM

30

How stonehenge was built

Stonehenge is one of the most remarkable achievements of prehistoric engineering in Europe. For building it the only motive power was human muscles, aided by the simplest devices such as ropes, levers and rollers.

The ditch, the Aubrey and the Y and Z Holes, and all the other holes for stones and posts were dug with pick-axes made from the antlers of red deer. The chalk rubble loosened with picks was scraped together with the shoulderblades of cattle and loaded into baskets so that it could be dumped where required. Wooden shovels may have been used as well, but no trace of them survives. Modern experiments have shown that these tools are more effective than they look. To dig the Stonehenge ditch and build the bank with them would have taken only twice the time required to do it today with steel picks, shovels and buckets.

The bluestones at Stonehenge certainly come from the Preseli Mountains in south-west Wales and from the shores of Milford Haven. Whether they were brought directly to Stonehenge, or to some intermediate point in the first instance, their transport over so long a distance is an astonishing feat. The map shows the most likely route. From the Preseli Mountains, where boulders of bluestone of all shapes and sizes lie on the surface, they would be dragged on sledges and rollers to the headwaters of Milford Haven. There they would be loaded on to rafts, and carried by water along the south coast of Wales and up the Rivers Avon and Frome to near the modern town of Frome in Somerset. On the rivers, boats were probably used instead of rafts, which would have run aground in shallow water. From there they would be hauled overland again for about 10km (6 miles) to near Warminster in Wiltshire. Not far away there is a long barrow called Bowls Barrow in which a large block of bluestone has been found, built in to a central core of boulders. This long barrow was almost certainly constructed before 2900BC, so that at least some bluestones must have arrived in the neighbourhood by that date. From here to Stonehenge the route is again mainly by water, down the River Wylye to Salisbury and up the Salisbury Avon to West Amesbury. The total distance along this route is about 385km (240 miles).

The sarsen stones were almost certainly brought from the Marlborough Downs near Avebury in north Wiltshire, about 30km (20 miles) north of Stonehenge, where large blocks of the stone lie thickly on the surface. For these heavier stones water transport would be impossible, and they must have been dragged overland all the way on massive sledges and rollers, hauled with ropes of leather or cow-hair. The map shows the most

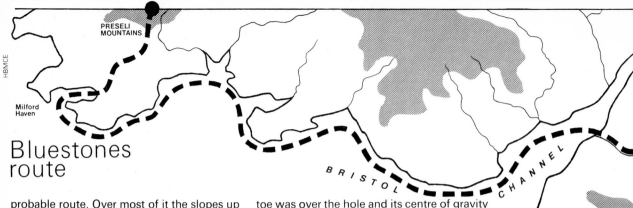

PRESELI
MOUNTAINS

Milford
Haven

Bluestones route

B R I S T O L   C H A N N E L

probable route. Over most of it the slopes up and down are fairly easy; but at Redhorn Hill on the southern edge of the Vale of Pewsey the gradient is steep. To pull the heaviest stone, weighing about 50 tonnes, up this hill would have needed about 500 men, with an extra hundred at least to lay the rollers in front of the sledge and keep it from wandering sideways. Altogether the transport of about 80 sarsen stones over this distance probably occupied a thousand men for several years.

At Stonehenge itself the uprights and lintels were dressed to shape by pounding their surfaces with heavy sarsen hammers about the size of a football, many of which were later used as packing-stones round the bases of the uprights. The hollow mortices in the lintels were made in the same way. The tops of the stones must have been dressed level, leaving the tenons projecting, only after the uprights had been raised and given time to settle in the chalk. This was slow work, because sarsen stone is exceptionally hard and will turn the cutting edge even of modern steel tools.

The method probably used to erect the stones is shown opposite. A foundation pit was dug in the chalk, with one side vertical and the opposite one in the form of a sloping ramp. A row of wooden stakes was driven in against the vertical side to stop the chalk being crushed down by the toe of the stone as it was raised. The stone, base foremost, was then moved on rollers towards the ramp, until its

toe was over the hole and its centre of gravity was just behind the leading roller (1). The outer end was then levered up, dipping the base into the hole, until the stone over-balanced at the last moment and came to rest in a leaning position. Next, with levers supported by timber packing (2), it was raised a few inches at a time and held in place by struts when the packing had to be rebuilt closer to the stone (3). Finally it would be pulled upright by gangs of men hauling on ropes. To raise a stone of the outer circle of sarsens would need about 200 men.

To help in adjusting the stones to a vertical position, their bases were dressed to a blunt point on which the mass could more easily pivot. When the final adjustment had been made, the hole round the base was rapidly packed with stones, including discarded hammers, and with chalk rammed hard (4).

The method probably used to raise the lintels is shown below. First the lintel is positioned on the ground, close and parallel to the base of the uprights, and each end alternately is lifted with levers and supported on temporary packing of squared timber (1). Then a 'crib' of criss-crossed timbers is built around the lintel and uprights (2), and decked over with stout planks just beneath the underside of the lintel. Now the weight of the stone is transferred with levers from the old packing resting on the ground to new packing resting on the deck (3). Thereafter the whole process

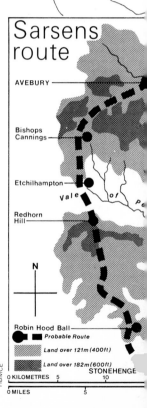

Sarsens route

AVEBURY

Bishops
Cannings

Etchilhampton

Vale   of   Pe

Redhorn
Hill

N

Robin Hood Ball
■—■ Probable Route

▨ Land over 121m (400ft)

▩ Land over 182m (600ft)

STONEHENGE

0 KILOMETRES   5   10

0 MILES   5

ising the sarsens

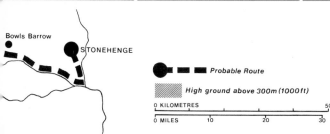

Bowls Barrow
STONEHENGE

● ━ ━ ━ **Probable Route**

▨ **High ground above 300m (1000ft)**

0 KILOMETRES   50

0 MILES   10   20   30

is repeated in stages, the lintel being raised about 60cm (2ft) at each stage (4). Finally when the uppermost deck was level with the tops of the uprights the lintel is levered sideways to fit over the projecting tenons (5). Once it was in place the crib would have been dismantled for re-use. Lifting in this way has been used by modern engineers in places abroad where no machines were available.

Above: four stages of raising a sarsen to an upright position

osite and above: the route of the bluestones Preseli. A large tone boulder was found wls Barrow

probable route of the sarsens the Marlborough Downs

Below: five stages of lifting a lintel to the top of a trilithon

ising the lintels

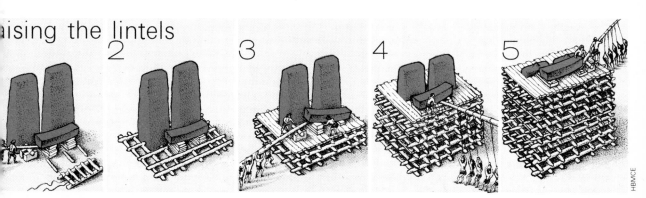

woodhenge

Woodhenge lies about 3km (2 miles) to the north-east of Stonehenge, just to the west of the A345. It was formerly supposed to be the site of a destroyed disc-barrow (p38) ; but air-photographs taken in 1925 showed rings of dark spots in the crop of wheat growing over it, suggesting that there were holes under-ground in which wooden posts had stood. This was confirmed when the site was excavated soon afterwards. The positions of the wooden posts are now marked by concrete blocks.

The outer boundary consisted of a circular bank, now almost flattened by ploughing, with a broad flat-bottomed ditch inside it, originally about 2.5m (8ft) in depth, and an entrance-gap on the north-north-east side. This earthwork was built about 2300BC.

On the flat area inside the ditch the excavators found six concentric oval rings of circular holes, which had held wooden posts of varying size. The larger ones had sloping ramps cut into the chalk at the side, down which the bases of the posts had been slid when they were erected. Once upright, the holes and ramps were filled with tightly-rammed chalk.

Near the centre there was a grave containing the body of a three-year-old child whose skull had been split before burial (now marked by a small cairn of flints). This was perhaps a dedicatory burial, and is one of the very few pieces of evidence for human sacrifice in Neolithic Britain. South of it, in the second ring from the outside, an oblong concrete block marks a hole for an upright stone, which was probably of sarsen.

Since only their ground-plan is known, it is difficult to reconstruct these rings of posts with any certainty. They may have stood in the open, carved and painted, and perhaps with their tops joined by lintels at different levels, like the stones of Stonehenge. On the other hand, they may be the uprights of a roofed building. As the largest posts are in the third ring, this would probably have looked like a huge thatched barn bent round on itself, leaving an open space in the centre.

Whatever its original form, this timber struc-ture was probably a temple, a tribal meeting-place or a combination of both. The discovery of symbolic axe-heads carved out of soft chalk, buried in post-holes of the two outer rings at Woodhenge, hints at its use for a magical or religious purpose in which axes had a special meaning. The bronze axe-heads carved at Stonehenge (p26) show the long-continued use of the axe as a symbol.

Symbolic axe-heads of chalk, buried in post-holes at Woodhenge (Devizes Museum)

e plan of Woodhenge (right) shows the rings of
st-holes found inside the remains of the
thwork. The larger holes have ramps, to make it
ier to erect the posts. How the posts were used is
rely guess-work, but they make sense best as the
mework of a circular building. The thickest and
hest timbers would support the ridge of the roof,
d the eaves would rest on smaller posts on the
ide and outside, leaving an open light-well in the
tre. The illustration below shows a possible
onstruction of this building

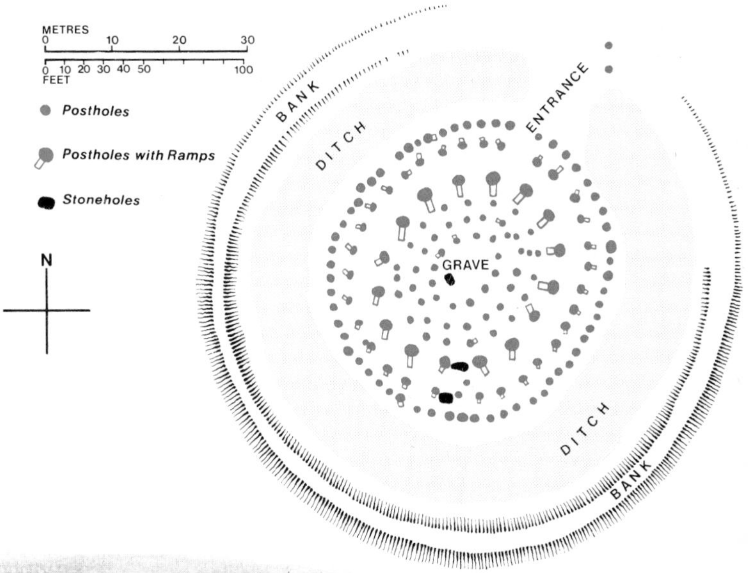

METRES
0   10   20   30
0 10 20 30 40 50   100
FEET

● Postholes

◖ Postholes with Ramps

◆ Stoneholes

N

BANK
DITCH
ENTRANCE
GRAVE
DITCH
BANK

Durrington walls

The earthwork of Durrington Walls lies immediately north of Woodhenge, spanning a dry valley. It has been much altered and damaged by ploughing in the past.

Originally it consisted of a huge, roughly oval bank of chalk, about 30m (100ft) wide at the base and 3m (10ft) high, built from material dug out of a ditch on the inside. This was up to 10m (33ft) wide and up to 6m (20ft) deep, with very steep sides and a flat bottom. There were entrances on opposite sides, the lower one being close to the River Avon. Both bank and ditch show curious kinks in their outlines, perhaps to avoid structures still standing. The site was first occupied from about 3200BC and the earthwork was built around 2550BC.

The strip of land beneath the embankment of the new road was excavated in 1966–68, and revealed the remains of two circular timber structures. The 'Northern Circle' may have been a round thatched building about 14.5m (48ft) across, with a roof raised in the centre to admit light and air. A fenced path led to it from the south, through another fence at right-angles. It was built about 2450BC, and may have replaced an earlier building of uncertain plan.

In the 'Southern Circle' there are also the remains of two successive buildings of timber. The earlier one was about 23m (75ft) in diameter. It may have been roofed right across; but more probably it had a ring-shaped roof sloping inwards, like that of a football-ground, enclosing an open space with a circle of posts, which could have been carved and painted. The later building had six circles of posts, the outer one being 39m (128ft) in diameter. It was built about 2450BC, and was probably roofed with an open space at the centre, like Woodhenge.

Durrington Walls, like Stonehenge, gives us an idea of the amount of labour devoted by the Late-Neolithic people of the area to 'public works'. To build the earthwork would require nearly a million man-hours, or 100 men working six days a week for four years. It cannot have been easy, either, to fell, transport and erect the large oak tree-trunks used in the timber buildings here and at Woodhenge. The largest of these were over 1m (3.3ft) in diameter and could have been up to 11m (36ft) in length. An unseasoned oak trunk of this size weighs nearly 11 tonnes.

This is less than half the weight of an average sarsen upright at Stonehenge; but such a post would be even longer than the tallest sarsen, and its centre of gravity would be even further from its lower end. In practical terms, the engineering problems overcome by the builders of these huge timber structures were probably no smaller than those which arose later in the raising of the Stonehenge sarsens. Indeed, the successful construction of the sarsens at Stonehenge, and the use of woodworking joints, probably owed a great deal to this previous working with long and heavy lengths of timber, rigidly fixed together.

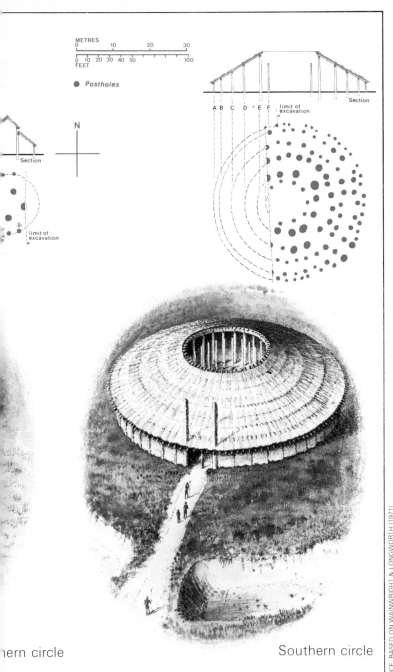

METRES
0   10   20   30

FEET
0 10 20 30 40 50   100

● Postholes

A B C D E F

limit of excavation

Section

Section

limit of excavation

ern circle

Southern circle

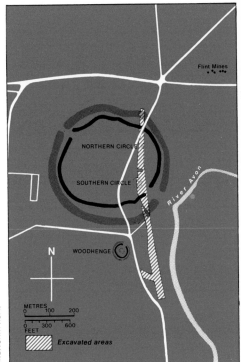

NORTHERN CIRCLE

SOUTHERN CIRCLE

Flint Mines

River Avon

WOODHENGE

N

METRES
0   100   200

FEET
0   300   600

⬚ Excavated areas

The map above shows the
positions of Woodhenge
and Durrington Walls, and
the River Avon

HBMCE. BASED ON WAINWRIGHT & LONGWORTH (1971)

HBMCE

The Round Barrows

All round Stonehenge the landscape is dotted with round barrows, the burial-mounds of the Beaker people and their successors in the Early Bronze Age. Many have now been flattened by ploughing, so that originally they were even more numerous than they appear today. Even now we can see more barrows within 3km (2 miles) of Stonehenge than in any other area of the same size in Britain.

Many of them are grouped in cemeteries strung out in a line along a ridge. One of the largest of these can be seen from Stonehenge on the crest of Normanton Down, 800m (0.5 miles) to the south. Another stands on the rising ground to the north-west, near the Cursus, and a third is concealed in the two beech woods on the skyline to the east, on either side of the course of the Avenue.

A well-preserved barrow-cemetery runs north-eastwards from the roundabout on the A303 at Winterbourne Stoke cross-roads 2.4km (1.5 miles) from Stonehenge. It contains examples of all the main kinds of round barrow to be found in the Stonehenge area. Those furthest from the cross-roads are simple bowl-shaped mounds, with or without a surrounding ditch, known as *bowl barrows*. These were used by the Beaker people, and continued into the Early Bronze Age, for the burials of both men and women. Nearer the cross-roads, close to the edge of the wood, there are two *bell barrows*, with the edge of the large mound separated from the surrounding ditch by a flat space. These belong to the Early Bronze Age, and seem always to cover the burials of men only.

Overlapping the ditch of the bell barrow nearer the cross-roads is a *pond barrow*, a rare type in which a central circular hollow is surrounded by a ring-shaped bank. Only about forty of these are known altogether, all of them in Wessex. Some contain burials; others enclose a flint pavement on which ceremonies to honour the near-by dead may have been conducted. They are perhaps the prehistoric counterpart of a medieval chantry or chapel attached to a family grave-yard.

North of the bell barrows, and outside the main line, there are two *disc barrows*, with small mounds surrounded at a distance by a ditch with an outer bank. These too belong to the Early Bronze Age, and seem always to contain the cremated burials of women. Near them to the north-east is a ditched bowl barrow and a second pond barrow, larger than the first.

The main line of barrows is on the axis of the earlier Neolithic long barrow close to the round-about. This suggests the continuous use of the same cemetery, over a period of 1500 years or more, for the burial of the most important members of some ruling family. The other barrow cemeteries in the area are probably of the same special kind, and cannot represent the burials of the population at large. It is clear that where barrows are set in a long straight line, the disc barrows always lie to one side. This is evidence, perhaps, for the

WEST AIR PHOTOGRAPHY

Below left: *aerial view of part of the cemetery of round barrows along the ridge of Normanton Down, 1km south of Stonehenge*

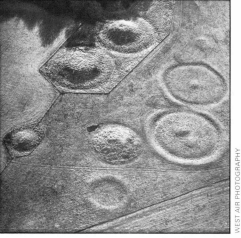

Above: *a closer view of barrows at Winterbourne Stoke cross-roads; on the left, a bowl and two bell barrows in line; right, two disc barrows; centre, a ditched bowl barrow and a pond barrow*

39

museums

separate position of women in the aristocracy of the Early Bronze Age.

Most of these barrows around Stonehenge were partially excavated at the beginning of the nineteenth century, and the objects deposited in the graves can be seen in the Devizes and Salisbury Museums. Men were often buried with weapons such as bronze daggers, bronze tomahawks and stone battle-axes, which can be regarded as symbols of rank and authority, like the sword worn by senior officers of the armed forces on special ceremonial occasions today. Women's graves contain bead necklaces and other ornaments. In Beaker times and at the beginning of the Early Bronze Age the bodies of the dead were usually buried in a crouched position in a grave cut in the chalk. Later the cremation of the body on a funeral pyre became increasingly common, and eventually universal, the burned ashes being deposited in a small pit or in a pottery urn before the barrow was heaped up over them. Sometimes later burials were inserted into the mounds of existing barrows, built at an earlier date.

In spite of their exceptional number, the barrows round Stonehenge can only be the burial-places of the leading members of the leading families in each generation – the ruling class who had the wealth and the power to command the transport and erection of the bluestones and the sarsens at Stonehenge. They are not the burials of the common people who did the work. Their only memorial is Stonehenge itself.

Museums where the objects shown in this book may be seen are credited in individual captions. Items from the Stonehenge excavations are mostly in the Salisbury and South Wilts Museum at 42 St Ann Street, Salisbury. Artefacts from barrows can be seen in the Devizes Museum of the Wiltshire Archaeological and Natural History Society at Long Street, Devizes. This museum has a display room devoted to henge monuments. Visitors are advised to check hours of admission in advance.

Amber discs, miniature halberds and horned pendant, all plated with gold, from Wessex graves (Devizes Museum)

Printed in the UK for HMSO 8820801. C500. 4/85. 42560